RIP OFF
THE REARVIEW
MIRROR

Chad J. Willett

Edited by Leonard Hayhurst

Rip Off the Rearview Mirror is dedicated to:

The passing of our father, Lynn H. Willett
My wife and daughter, Erika and Scarlett Willett
My mom, Mary Kay Willett

Cover Art Director: Aaron Buckley

Printed in the United States of America

First printing, 2018

ISBN 978-1-945091-57-5

Ordering information: Special discounts are available on quantity purchases by bookstores, corporations, associations, and others. For details, contact the publisher at:

sales@braughlerbooks.com
or at 937-58-BOOKS

For questions or comments about this book, please write to:

info@braughlerbooks.com

Braughler™
Books
braughlerbooks.com

Contents

4 Through Line: "Remember There Are No Small Parts, Only Small Actors" 33

5 Mindsets: "Orville Wright Didn't Have a Pilot's License" 45

"The only minute you can control is now.
Living in the past creates depression.
Living in the future creates anxiety.
We only have this moment to discover our
"Through Line" in life."

Anonymous Author

Introduction

It all began with a blog I posted on May 19, 2017:

What is your biggest regret? What do you wish you could have done over? Imagine how different your life would be if you accepted failure and moved on. That's right, I am not saying we will forget it, because we won't; however, we can accept it and move on.

Personally, I wish I would have spent 4 years in LA rather than 7. Spending 7 years in LA kept me from my family, friends, and starting a career. It is time I will never get back, and during those 3 extra years, I wasn't helping people. I was living solely for myself with no one else in mind.

In the past, I would give this regret time and attention; now I accept it as part of my journey and move on. I never think about my days in LA other than for fun. During the workday, all I am focused on are my businesses. That is it, I am laser-focused on my "To Do" list and getting things done.

How do you rip off the rearview mirror and never look back? You focus on the here and now, you determine your wants (short-term/long-term), and you go after them. When we aren't focused on the here and now and don't know what we want is when we wander. Wandering causes us to live in the past, dwell on our failures, and waste energy.

What is the rearview mirror? It symbolizes anything that takes us out of the present moment and takes our focus off our objectives. This includes living in the past, anticipating the future, and all the background "Noise" that surrounds us all.

When we reflect on the past, three things happen:

1. **Regrets:** Most of us who revisit the past have regrets and beat ourselves up about what could have been, or the decision we made and wish we had back.
2. **Distractions:** In our minds, we are re-constructing situations that happened a week ago, a month ago, or even years ago. It distracts

us from the tasks at hand and what we want to accomplish that hour and that day.

3. **Feelings:** The past generally brings up feelings of regret, loss, and disappointment.

When we think about the future, three things also happen:

1. **Anxiety:** When we think about what might or could happen, it increases our energy levels and causes unnecessary stress and anxiety.
2. **Lose the "Moment":** We become less present by thinking about events that may or may not happen.
3. **Faulty Vision:** We try to create a grand vision that is impossible to achieve, but that makes us feel important. However, these unrealistic goals add stress, anxiety, and take us out of our daily goals.

Instead of thinking about the past, or worrying about the future, "Rip Off the Rearview Mirror" by developing a "Through Line" in your life. The "Through Line" is comprised of your short-term and long-term objectives and gives you direction.

Objectives — Can be broken down into two categories:

- Short-term objectives: What we want in 1–3 years
- Long-term objectives: What we want in 3–5 years

Creating your "Through Line" in life allows you to "Rip Off the Rearview Mirror!" Imagine channeling your energies toward your "Wants," rather than on past regrets or the future. If right now, you give 20% of your time and efforts toward your short-term and long-term wants, imagine what giving 60%, 70%, or even 80% could accomplish.

Finally, there is another enemy to "Ripping Off the Rearview Mirror," and that is "Noise!" "Noise" is everything around us that distracts us from accomplishing our objectives: social media, advertisements, radio, TV, internet, and the hundreds of interruptions we experience each and every day. We will examine "Noise" in the next section, as it is our biggest enemy living in the 21st century.

Are you ready to "Rip Off the Rearview Mirror" and create a "Through Line" in your life?

Let's get to work!

1 NOISE
"A Cracked Mirror"

Whether it is at work, at home, or on the phone, we all want to be heard and relevant. However, it is difficult because "Noise" drowns us out; it is everywhere. "Noise" takes a hold of our lives and creates barriers, comfort, busyness, and a false sense of reality. The more "Noise" we listen to, the harder it is to "Rip Off the Rearview Mirror."

Most dangerously, "Noise" keeps us from creating a "Through Line" in our life and gets us off track. It takes our focus off our short-term and long-term goals. Many men and women who lack direction, struggle with addictions, and lack motivation do not have a "Through Line" in their life. Rather, they get caught up in the daily "Noise" and wander from job to job, relationship to relationship, and go through life not knowing what they truly want.

Do you want to wander through life? I did it for seven years while living in Los Angeles, chasing my dream of becoming an actor. However, I can tell you my life changed when I discovered my "Through Line." That is my goal for you, to discover your "Through Line" and get purpose back in your life, channel your energies toward your wants, and accomplish more than you ever thought was possible.

But first, let us take a closer look at "Noise."

Noise:

We are always anticipating what we are going to say next, which keeps us from being silent. Therefore, we become engaged in an endless stream of dialogue where both parties never stop to think, and are not able to absorb or process what is being said. Rather, the goal in our conversations is to talk, ask questions, and avoid silence.

However, by avoiding silence we don't allow ourselves or the other person the opportunity to:

- **Think:** Silence gives you a moment to think about what is being said.
- **Reflect:** Silence allows you to reflect on your answer, rather than responding emotionally and impulsively.
- **Absorb:** Silence allows you to absorb the information and content being delivered.

Next time you are in a conversation, see how many silent pauses you or the person you are talking to have during your discussion. If the answer is zero, ask yourself what did you get out of that conversation? Where you able to think, reflect, and absorb what was being communicated?

As a speaker, I have been trained to pause throughout my keynote addresses. Professional speakers say audiences must have time to think, reflect, and absorb when we are talking; otherwise, the information will never be processed.

Why can't we be silent? Because we feel we must always be talking (adding Noise) or asking questions to keep the conversation moving forward. You can't rip out the rearview mirror if you can't be silent. It is impossible, silence allows us to think, contemplate and escape the "Noise" that is around us.

CRACKED MIRROR

"My mind is constantly going. For me to completely relax, I gotta get rid of my cell phone."

—Kenny Chesney

Barriers

Randy Pausch, a computer science professor at Carnegie Mellon University, gave a presentation called the "Last Lecture" shortly after he was diagnosed with terminal cancer. During the presentation, he talks about how bricks (barriers) keep people from achieving their dreams.

Pausch's last talk was about the importance of overcoming obstacles, of enabling the dreams of others, and seizing every moment. He didn't talk about dying. He talked about the importance of achieving your childhood dreams.

We all have barriers that keep us from doing what we love and keep many of us from tapping into our passions and reaching our full potential. But, if we want to break free from the barriers, we must have the will and determination to go after what we want. The stronger our will, the greater the chance we will have at overcoming these obstacles.

How bad do you want something? Because, if you don't want something bad enough, living in the past will work for you. However, if you want to excel, and be great at what you do, living in the present moment is the only way this is going to happen. Those who want it bad enough will break through the bricks and achieve their goals and aspiration in life.

On the other side of the coin, those who don't want it bad enough will be stopped by the bricks and deterred from their dreams, passions, and wants. What are your dreams? Once you determine your wants in life, the next question is what bricks are in your way?

During our journey, we will come across many negative people who will add to our "Noise" by telling us not to try something new, take a risk, or break through a barrier. Many times, these are the people who never made it through their own walls and don't want you to make it through yours. But it is our will and determination that will allow us to overcome barriers and get what we want out of life.

CRACKED MIRROR

"It was satisfying to take a risk and see it pay off."

—Kenny Chesney

The "Box" of Life

We live in a time where we get "Boxed" in by labels! It appears we are our job title, nothing more, and nothing less. It is all part of branding, image control, and specializing. We limit ourselves to the job we do, and the title associated with it.

Recently, my wife and I began flipping houses — something outside my proverbial "Box of Life." I am an artist, not a real estate person. I have been told not to blog about real estate, not to put it on my website, and to keep it separate from my speaking business.

Why have I been told that? The answer is clear, what could a man who has spent his whole life in the arts know about real estate? When I began flipping houses, I didn't know anything about it. I am not an expert, yet, but I am learning as I go. That is the mindset I want to embrace: learn as I go, make mistakes, experiment, explore, and have successes. This is the entrepreneurial spirit we all have, and we all should embrace; but, for many of us it has been distinguished.

I am not promoting quitting your job, or starting a new business or a side business. Rather, I am suggesting we broaden the way we think about our job and responsibilities. We can do more than our job title, and this includes having meetings with people outside our department, getting involved in events that are opposite our specialization, and taking on roles that are outside our normal everyday procedures.

The most creative men and women I know don't specialize; rather, they are open to new opportunities and experiences that are outside their job description.

Are you boxed in?

Cruise Control

When we are on "Cruise Control," we do what we have always done: Looking in the rearview mirror and coasting. This happened to me in 2017 when a former client brought me back to speak to her managers in Columbus, Ohio. I did the same keynote address I had given two years before, this time to a different audience. When she and I met at Max & Erma's for lunch, she had two pages of notes for me, which included:

- My performance this time was negative.
- The talk was lower-energy.
- I was showing videos to fill time and space.
- I didn't get the audience to participate.
- I need to read more and own my space.
- I was self-indulgent.
- I need to stop referencing Steve Jobs.
- I need to use artist to make my point

If we hadn't had that lunch, I would have continued to do the "Smash the Box" keynote address the way I had done it the prior two years: Lower energy, negative tone, not reading and getting innovative ideas, and in short, coasting from performance to performance.

Yes, hearing this fierce feedback was tough; it was fierce; however, it was honest! A lot of what this woman said to me was true even if it was hard to hear. This is what happens when we live in the past and seek comfort rather than truth; it allows us to operate in a false reality.

And since getting this feedback, I have taken my speaking career to another level. My last three keynote addresses have been higher energy, with more audience engagement, and a clearer message. Recently, I presented to the teachers at a charter school in Columbus, Ohio. When I finished the presentation, the school's director was blown away at how much I had improved as a speaker.

The result? She wants to co-write a book with me next year on presentation skills for teachers in the classroom. This would have never been possible if I hadn't had that fierce conversation with my co-worker at the restaurant. If she hadn't been brutally honest with me, I wouldn't have known what to improve and how to get better.

When we coast, we are listening to the "Noise" around us and doing what we have always done in the past. Being defensive and sensitive are ways to disengage from fierce and difficult conversations.

People who are sensitive and defensive rarely hear the truth. Let's be honest, who wants to engage people in these conversations if they are going to attack you and/ or go on the defensive? It is easier to allow them to coast through life and do what they have always done.

You have to decide — do you want to be on autopilot looking back into the rearview mirror? Or, do you want to get your life off of cruise control by being open to fierce conversations and making changes?

CRACKED MIRROR

"I'll admit I am a workaholic."

—Kenny Chesney

Being Busy

Busyness is "Noise!" The busier we are, the better. Isn't that what we have always thought? But, is it right? The busier we are, the more distracted we become. We rush to decisions, produce mediocre performance, and lack creativity.

Is your calendar filled Monday through Friday from 8:00 a.m. to 5:00 p.m.? If not filled, is it full? We negate ourselves the opportunity to be creative at work by filling up our day with endless meetings, conference calls, and appointments. The question is do you ever have time to be present during your day?

We are constantly thinking about our next meeting, conference call, or to-do list item that disconnects us from being present. We keep ourselves forever out of the moment by overscheduling ourselves and having the NEXT thing to think about.

Creative thinking requires us to be fully engaged in the present moment to idea generate and problem-solve. Working America does not have a problem with being efficient, managing time, or productivity; however, it does have a problem with ideas and solutions.

Being busy stops the flow of idea generation. We don't leave ourselves any time in our meetings to brainstorm, come up with a new concept or service, because we don't have the time. We must get our "To Do" list done and accomplish as much as possible during our day if it is to be a success. How can we create new ideas if we don't have the time to do it?

Most groups and companies are better at problem-solving than idea generating; however, being busy also limits this ability. To solve problems takes time, and again, if we are always busy, we don't have that time. That is why companies repeatedly tell me they rarely have problem solvers, instead they have people who report the problem but don't come up with the solution.

What does your calendar look like? How are you managing your time? Is it filled with "Noise"?

CRACKED MIRROR:

"I want to spend more time with my family."

—Kenny Chesney

A False Reality

Listening to "Noise" creates a false reality! It is a reality based on consumption! Buy things, and your life will get better! Buy that new house, sweater, car, or blouse and you will feel better. That is what "Noise" wants us to do; it wants to distract us from our objectives and "Through Line" in life and think that happiness, contentment, and purpose are achieved by buying something bigger, better, and nicer.

I have fallen victim to it. My wife and I bought a new house in the suburbs of Columbus, Ohio, and I had to buy in one of the nicest areas of Columbus. My ego is large, and subconsciously, I told myself if I bought a house in a great area with a great reputation that it would fill my ego. Yes, I too can fall victim to "Noise" and consumption.

However, I discovered my "Through Line" in life. My "Through Line" helps me guard against all the distractions I come across each and every day. I rarely shop for myself, I throw away all mailers that tell us to buy more, I drive a modest car, and do everything in my power to stay grounded and know that if I want a purposeful life, I must keep my eye on the "Through Line" of life.

We aren't always aware that the "Noise" going on around us is distracting us from accomplishing our objectives and super objectives in life and creating a "Through Line." Being on guard of "Noise" is a 24/7 battle!

CRACKED MIRROR

"I think in the last four or five years I have struggled with the balance in my life."

—Kenny Chesney

CHAPTER SUMMARY
A Cracked Mirror

A "Cracked Mirror" is full of Noise and includes:

1. *Distractions* — We don't have time to think, contemplate, and give heavy thought to the issues that are in front of us. We just go from one activity to the next.

2. *Negativity* — Naysayers gain a stronger voice in our lives.

3. *Cruise Control* — We do what we have always done in our lives, and hope for different results.

4. *Busyness* — We keep forever busy, hoping things will change and our lives will get better.

5. *False Reality* — We live in a reality of consumption rather than contentment.

There is hope! As you will discover in this book, when you create a "Through Line" in your life, your reality will be based on truth rather than lies. It will be based on results, not propaganda. Let us begin building our "Through Line" in life and begin with objectives.

OBJECTIVES

"Where our focus goes... Energy Flows"

Tony Robbins said, "Where our focus goes…Energy flows." And we need our energy and our focus on our objectives if we are to "Rip Off the Rearview Mirror." Think of objectives as goals, and when we have defined them we can focus on them and channel all our energies toward them. When we don't define our objectives, we flounder, we lose direction, and we get caught up in the "Noise" of life.

Tony Robbins has had a career that has spanned decades, and his success can be partially tied to his ability to define his objectives. Watch his documentary "I'm Not Your Guru," and you will see a man that was meant to speak. It is his passion, his energy source, and destiny to influence the lives of those he comes in contact with.

Give yourself time to think this through and define your objectives, because they will define you. Your objectives, or lack of objectives, will have a major impact on the career you have, the relationships you hold, and the journey you take. Remember, where our focus goes, energy flows, and the question is does it flow toward an objective or does it flow toward "Noise?"

Knowing your objectives in life allows you to become unbalanced, create a positive mindset, grow, and become problem-solvers. All of these attributes are desperately needed in a time when "Noise" distracts us and keeps us from doing what we are meant to do with the life we live. Only when we know what we want out of life can we gain direction, purpose, and a live up to our God-given potential.

Let us begin constructing your "Through Line" in life by defining your objectives.

Objectives

Simon Sinek made knowing your "Why" very popular during his TED Talk presentation. I want to go one step further, the "Why" is important, but just as important is the "Want." What do we want out of life, our objectives (short-term wants) and super objectives (long-term wants)?

The clearer we are on our "Wants," the more likely we are to find happiness, success, enjoyment, and fulfillment. Very few people take the time to figure out their short term or long term "Wants." Without these wants, we are boats without rudders. We are lost out at sea without direction or a plan to accomplish our goals.

You should define your short term and long term objectives. My short term objectives are ones for the next one to three years. I want to be an international speaker, flip houses with wife and partner my acting studio with a local theater company.

Objective (1–3 year goals): I want to be an international speaker.

Objective (1–3 year goals): I want to flip two houses a year with my wife.

Objective (1–3 year goals): I want to partner up my acting studio with a local theater company in Columbus, Ohio, called CATCO.

Once you define your wants, all your focus and energy will go toward that goal. For example, in order to be an international speaker, I have to channel my energies on a daily basis to achieve this goal. First, I know I need to create original content each and every week. Therefore, I write a weekly blog, I film backstage videos when I am speaking and put them on social media, and I'm working on new books.

In 2017, my wife and I flipped our first house and we are waiting on the bank to purchase our second flipped house this year. In order to prepare for our second flip, I am getting a crew together to do carpet, paint, windows, lawn care and general maintenance. In addition, my wife and I are looking at houses that sell in the area we are buying and seeing how they are designed and staged in order to get new ideas. Finally, we have a home equity line of credit in place to help pay for the renovations.

I have had my acting studio for 9 years, and we are joining forces with a theater company in Columbus, called CATCO. Starting in January of 2018, I will be running the back end of my studio (marketing, enrollment, and payroll), but I won't be teaching any classes. The strategy behind this line of thinking is to channel my focus on my two short-term objectives: International Speaker/Flipping houses.

Can you see how defining your objectives channels your energies and guides your focus? My focus all day is on my speaking business, my acting studio, and flipping houses. Are your objectives clearly defined? If the answer is "No," most likely you are wasting energy, time, and precious resources every day by not defining what you want.

WHERE OUR FOCUS GOES...ENERGY FLOWS

"Setting goals is the first step in turning the invisible into the visible."
–Tony Robbins

Begin "Ripping Off the Rearview Mirror" by going to the back of the book and defining your objectives.

Unbalance = Success[1]

Defining our objectives allows us to become "Unbalanced" in life. When we are unbalanced in life is when we gain energy. Everyone strives for a work/life balance these days; however, when we are out of balance that is when we do great things.

My current obsession is real estate, and this has me off-balance. I am trying to read, study, and master the art of flipping properties to the best of my ability. I don't want to take my time and be balanced; I want to be unbalanced and throw myself completely into these projects.

Some would say that is risky and irresponsible, but, I would say it is passion. It is what I enjoy doing, and I want to immerse myself in it. When people find their passions, that is when they become unbalanced, break their patterns and routines, and become energized.

If we want to immerse ourselves in our work, our job, or our cause, we must become imbalanced and go all in. This is how we will make our mark on the people we come in contact with each and every day.

---

[1] This blog came from an "Unplanned Collaboration" with Ken Lazar at Ability Professional Staffing.

"Whatever happens, take responsibility."

–Tony Robbins

Changing the Words You Use: "I am the greatest"

Muhammad Ali clearly defined his objectives in life:

1. Be the greatest boxer of all time
2. Speak his mind openly and honestly in the political arena
3. Use his fame to promote causes that affect mankind

He then began using words that supported his objectives in life that increased his confidence, self-esteem, and gave him energy. When interviewed, Ali said he kept telling himself and others that he is the "greatest" hoping that it would come true someday. And sure enough it did, but where the power lies are the words he used to describe himself: greatest, champ, butterfly, fast, make medicine sick, etc.

The words we use to describe ourselves have a huge impact on our self-esteem, confidence, and our successes and failures in life. The more we believe in ourselves and our abilities, the greater the chance we have of being more successful, having meaningful relationships, and conquering the battles we want to conquer.

Ali had an incredible talent, work ethic, and charisma; however, he wouldn't have had the success he had if he hadn't used the words he used. There is something to be said about saying things out loud and having them come to fruition. When we tell people we have value, we add value; when we tell people we should be loved and respected, we are loved and respected.

We become framed by the words we use, both positively and negatively. It is like a self-fulfilling prophecy, if we believe in ourselves and our abilities we will begin to have successes. However, if we don't believe in ourselves and our abilities, and if we use negative words to describe ourselves, that too becomes our reality. Again, think of Ali, everything he says about himself is positive:

10. "I am the greatest. I said that even before I knew I was."

9. "I'm not the greatest, I'm the double greatest."

8. "It's not bragging if you can back it up."

7. "It's just a job. Grass grows, birds fly, waves pound the sand. I beat people up."

6. "I'm so mean, I make medicine sick."

5. "A man who views the world the same at 50 as he did at 20 has wasted 30 years of his life."

4. "Impossible is just a big word thrown around by small men who find it easier to live in the world they've been given than to explore the power they have to change it. Impossible is not a fact. It's an opinion. Impossible is not a declaration. It's a dare. Impossible is potential. Impossible is temporary. Impossible is nothing."

3. "If you even dream of beating me you'd better wake up and apologize."

2. "Don't count the days; make the days count."

1. "Float like a butterfly, sting like a bee. His hands can't hit what his eyes can't see. Now you see me, now you don't. George thinks he will, but I know he won't."

Once you define your objectives, begin looking at the words you use to describe yourself. Do the words you use re-enforce your short-term goals? For example, I want to be an international speaker, and here are the words I use to describe myself:

10. I am the greatest motivational speaker in Columbus, Ohio.

9. I can inspire hundreds of people at one time.

8. I get audiences engaged.

7. I bring more energy to my talks than any other speaker.

6. I get audiences to laugh.

5. I connect with groups of people.

4. I am prepared by practicing my material beforehand.

3. I entertain.

2. I get audiences to think and act different.

1. I inspire greatness.

As you can see, my list is much different than Muhammad Ali's. Take for example number 10 on my list: I am the greatest motivational speaker in Columbus, Ohio. I wanted to say the greatest motivational speaker in the country, but I don't believe it. I don't even believe I am the greatest motivational speaker in the state of Ohio.

Do you see my problem here? I am not using strong enough words or statements to support my objective of being an international speaker. And that is why I am not an international speaker yet—because my mind isn't right and I am not using words to justify that position. Only by writing this down do I see that I have to change the words I use to describe myself if I want to become an elite/international speaker.

After you define your objectives, examine the words you use to describe yourself. There will be a direct correlation between those words and your successes and failures. Muhammad Ali is a great example of this!

WHERE OUR FOCUS GOES...ENERGY FLOWS

"Live with passion."

–Tony Robbins

Expanding Your Tent

Channeling all your energies toward your objectives allows for expansion! Isn't that what it is all about — expanding, conquering, and growing? Whether we own, work for, or manage a business, we all want to expand our presence, our market share and move up the corporate ladder.

I have been professionally speaking for four and a half years, and I expanded my speaking business more than a 100 percent between years three and four. And I am talking revenue; the amount of money I charge for my keynote addresses/workshops has gone up substantially. The reason being I have clearly defined my objectives in life, which is to be an international speaker and a real estate mogul. That is it, as you can see, I am really only focused on two of my short-term objectives in that I am transitioning my Broadway2LA Acting Studio to CATCO in 2018.

This wasn't always the case for me. Before I met my wife, I was all over the board. I would start and stop businesses, never stick with any one job for more than a year or two, and always chase my next big idea. My wife brought to my attention my inability to focus and define my objectives, and I listened to her. We have been married for four years, and each year I have been with her, I have become more and more focused on my objectives.

And with this focus has come success and expansion. In 2017, I spoke in San Francisco, California; Boston, Massachusetts; Chicago, Illinois; and in and around the state of Ohio. Prior to 2017, I had never spoken on either coast, and I primarily spoke only in the state of Ohio. Again, this expansion is made possible by knowing what I want and going after it.

However, we must be on guard against the idea of expanding for expanding's sake. I started Broadway2LA Acting Studio in Columbus, Ohio, and within two years I expanded it to Cleveland and Cincinnati. I was in such a hurry to conquer new land and expand it that in the process, I wasn't prepared. I didn't have the infrastructure in place, the instructors, the website, or the marketing plan. As a result, all three markets suffered, and my enrollments went down in each market.

Expanding to expand can result in a bad investment decision. I expanded my acting studio too soon, and I wasn't ready to take on new business. After just 2 years in Cleveland and Cincinnati, I decided to shut down both locations and focus on Columbus. This has been one of the best business decisions I have made. As a result, all my efforts have been on improving the company and brand in one market. By focusing only on Columbus, I have grown market share, and improved the students' experience, and all facets of marketing — flyers, online advertising, website, etc.

WHERE OUR FOCUS GOES...ENERGY FLOWS

"In life you need either inspiration or desperation."
—Tony Robbins

Kicking Out the Ladder

Soichoro Honda (Founder of Honda) personally experienced numerous crisis and unexpected setbacks in his early years in the auto industry which included:

1. Factory destroyed by fire
2. Supplies rationed during wartime
3. Designs failed and threw productions schedules into a panic

While the crises weren't welcomed, Honda began to note how each crisis improved the eventual outcome. Over time, Honda came to value uncertainty as a catalyst for breakthroughs — so much so that he implemented a management practice that became known as "Kick Out the Ladder."

Just as a team neared completion on a project, he would create a crisis that would threaten everything. For example, if a team's deadline to finish a project was eight weeks, he would shorten the deadline to seven weeks. Creating this crisis forced his team to improvise and begin creating and innovating. He wanted his team to get away from thinking this is "how things have always been done" and think of new solutions, processes, and procedures.

I kicked out the ladder five years ago when I left corporate America and became an entrepreneur. I worked in corporate America for four years, and it had its advantages; Good pay, insurance, 401 K, vacation time, and stability.

However, I decided to create my own mini-crisis and leave corporate America and all its comforts. This decision caused me to completely focus on my acting studio, Broadway2LA, and a couple of years later begin motivational speaking. If I hadn't kicked out the ladder, I would still be working in corporate America and doing my acting studio only as a side business.

Again, only by being clear on my objectives in life was I able to make this decision. I knew that I wanted to give all my time and attention to my students: kids/teens/adults. The idea that I could inspire them in the classroom gave me energy and filled me up inside. Furthermore, it lead me to my ultimate passion of motivational speaking. As long as I can remember I wanted to speak.

Even as a teen in Zanesville, Ohio, I thought it would be so cool to be on stage like Tony Robbins, or Zig Ziglar to move and inspire individuals. Where I am at this point in my life wasn't achieved through comfort and doing things that were safe and predictable; rather the opposite: Kicking out the ladder and taking a leap of faith that it will all work out.

"The quality of your life is the quality of your relationships."
—Tony Robbins

Problem Solving

People who know what they want (objectives) solve problems. Doctors solve our health problems, lawyers solve our legal problems, counselors help solve mental problems, and leaders solve problems at work.

If we reframe our thinking and seek to solve problems rather than report them, we will be seen in a different mindset. I have had to shift my thinking on problem-solving in that I have been conditioned to bring problems up, not solve them. However, being a motivational speaker, I have realized that I am paid to not only motivate, but to solve problems.

For example, one of my talks, "Masks," deals with negativity in the workplace. I reduce negativity in the workplace by focusing on internal and external fires. Internal fires include making assumptions and taking things personally (we create these in our minds), while external fires are created through poor non-verbal communication. When groups finish the keynote address, they have solutions on how to reduce negativity in the workplace.

Once I decided I wanted to be a motivational speaker, I purposefully constructed talks that would help groups solve problems. For example, my top four keynote addresses are:

- "Smash the Box" — Creativity
- "Mindsets" — Creative leadership practices
- "Unleash the Guerrilla" — Guerrilla marketing strategies
- "Masks" — Negativity in the workplace

Each keynote address is constructed to solve problems. For example, "Smash the Box" solves the problem of a lack of creative thinking in the workplace by creating a culture of innovation. "Mindsets" solves the problem of a lack of creative leaders by giving audiences the tools to think, look, and act like a creative leader. "Unleash the Guerrilla" solves the problem of having a limited budget by using guerrilla marketing strategies. Finally, "Masks" solves the problem of reducing negativity in the workplace by improving the way we communicate non-verbally.

Successful men and women solve problems, it's what they are paid to do. Once we clearly know what we want and what we can do, we can begin solving problems.

WHERE OUR FOCUS GOES...ENERGY FLOWS

"We aren't in an information age, we are in entertainment age."
—Tony Robbins

CHAPTER SUMMARY

Where our focus goes...Energy Flows

Productivity blogger Merlin Mann calculated that on average we work an eight hour day, 50 weeks per year, and check our email every five minutes — just to see if anything new is in there. This means we check our email about 24,000 times a year. That isn't responding to emails, but only checking to see if we received new email in our inbox. Over the course of a year, he calculated that would work out to 66.6 hours a year of wasted time (Source: "The Accidental Creative"– by Todd Henry).

I not only check my emails at work; I also check my:

- Stock Quotes
- Delete
- Missed Calls

Each time I check my inbox, a stock quote, or my phone, I lose focus on writing my blog, working on my second book, or making calls to clients. The problem isn't just getting distracted, once distracted we have to re-channel our focus. Researchers say it takes anywhere form 1–3 minutes to get your focus back on a project.

How do we stay focused and not get distracted? I keep a note pad with my "To Do" list on it, and throughout the day I am constantly adding and subtracting items from it. The more organized my sheet of paper is, the less likely I am to get distracted. It is easy to drift, lose focus, and waste time and energy when we don't have a plan or strategy.

My notepad is a metaphor for my canvas and is similar to an artist who paints. This is my canvas I use every day to accomplish the objectives and super objective I have defined for my life. Everything that is on my notepad are immediate goals for that day, which tie into my objectives and super objectives in my life.

I am looking at it right now, and I have three columns on my note pad:

1. Column #1: My "To Do" list for my speaking business
2. Column #2: My "To Do" for immediate action items that day
3. Column #3: My "To Do" list for Broadway2LA Acting Studio

What does your note pad look like? How organized is your "To Do" list?

You have begun constructing your "Through Line" in life, now let us look at your super objective.

3

SUPER OBJECTIVE

"Unleashing Your Inner Michelangelo"

Once we define our super objective in life, we will unleash our inner Michelangelo by channeling all of our energies and focus toward our ultimate objective in life. Think of our inner "Michelangelo" as energy; when we define our ultimate objective, we will have an incredible amount of energy to tackle new projects, do what we do on a daily basis better, and accomplish more.

Michelangelo's super objective was to be the greatest artist he could be. This is what gave him the energy to work day and night on pieces of rocks that he turned into sculptures. And we must be very clear that we can have multiple objectives; however, we have one super objective. We don't think of Michelangelo as a politician, investor, and a merchant. No, we think of him as an artist, and that is where he spent all of his time, energy, and talents.

If we want to unleash our inner Michelangelo, we must define our super objective in life. Many of us will never sculpt, paint, speak, or create the next I-Phone. Yet, if we do what we love and do it with purpose, we will make a difference. And not just a difference, but we will gain direction and energy in our day-to-day activities.

Once you are doing what you love, your life will open up and you will create masterpieces like Michelangelo. Granted, they may not be chiseled from a rock, but, they will be your creation and authentic to you. You will gain energy, abandon autopilot, think differently, and dream again about what you love and are meant to do.

Let us finish creating your "Through Line" in life by defining your super objective, that will allow you to "Rip Off the Rearview Mirror."

Super Objective

Knowing your immediate wants (objective) gives you energy, while knowing your long-term want (super objective) sustains it. My wife and I go to St. Mary's Church in German Village, in Columbus, Ohio and we admire our deacon, Roger Minner. Deacon Minner is a great man and admired by the German Village Community. His super objective is to serve God.

He once told me that God has called him to serve in the church, and that is what he is doing. His super objective came from his Lord and he is doing the Lord's work. And as a result, all his actions are fueled by his super objective:

1. He assists mass on Saturday and Sundays.
2. He prepares couples for marriage.
3. He baptizes children.
4. He helps raise money for the church.
5. He volunteers at endless events put on by the church throughout the year.

Deacon Minner prepared my wife and I for marriage, and he also baptized our daughter Scarlett. We simply admire this man and what he stands for. Even deeper, we admire his ultimate purpose in life, which is to serve his Lord. His super objective in life is defined and that is what we love about him.

Many of us may not have faith and a super objective like Minner, but it's vital to take time to think and reflect on what our ultimate purpose in life is. Is it to help people, educate people, make money, donate our time and energies, build a company, or give back to your local community? Whatever it is, we need to define it and act on it; otherwise, we run into the danger of drifting and living a life without direction.

I lived seven years in Los Angeles chasing my dream of becoming a professional actor. I was young at 22 years old, and I thought my super objective was to be a professional actor. But I had no idea what that meant, the sacrifice it took, and what actually went into this craft.

However, the last four years in LA, I lost focus of my super objective, and I drifted. For example, I stopped waiting tables and going on auditions and began substitute teaching. Being a substitute teacher paid much better than waiting tables and allowed me to qualify for insurance. At this point in my life it was the most money I ever made.

Still, I wasn't acting! I was living a lie in that I told people I was a professional actor, but I wasn't doing anything to work on my craft: classes, workshops, head shots, resumés, or networking. During these four years of my life, I had no idea what my super objective in life was, and I floundered. I went through the motions of substitute teaching, occasionally went on an audition every couple of weeks, and socialized with my friends on the weekends.

This is what happens when we don't define our super objective; we lose direction and purpose. We either live in a false reality, or we wander and drift through life. There is a direct connection between what we want, and what we do in our actions. If we don't know what we want clearly and succinctly, we wander and drift through life.

Now, I am in my early forties and I have taken the time to define my super objective which is to influence people over the next five to 10 years of my life.

Super Objective (5–10 years goal): Influence people's lives

Yes, that is my super objective in life to be an inspirational/motivational speaker who influences people's lives. I am also honest with myself in that I am not planning on changing people's lives, or being their guru. Rather, I am blessed to think that I can have some influence on the way they think and act after hearing me talk.

As a result, I have put the majority of my focus on my speaking business. I write a weekly blog that I share on social media, I film videos of me "backstage" at my speaking events that I share with audiences, and I am working on new books based on blog posts and talks I deliver.

Knowing my super objective has given me direction in my life that I missed for so many years. I joke with my wife that after I met her, I got direction in my life, but it is true. Before I met her, I feel like I was always drifting from job to job, career to career and never knowing what I wanted out of life. My super objective before I met my wife was always about me. It wasn't about helping people, serving a higher power, or influencing the way people think. It was all about me, and that is not a way I want to live my life anymore.

I urge you to take the time and discover your super objective in life because it could change the course of it. You can write it down on a sheet of paper, think about it on your walks or jogs, or seek professional help and see a counselor who can help you discover it. It doesn't matter how you come to it, rather, what matters is that you have purpose and direction in your life by knowing what your ultimate goal is.

UNLEASHING YOUR INNER MICHELANGELO

"Every block of stone has a statue inside it and it is the task of the sculptor to discover it."

—Michelangelo

Continue "Ripping Off the Rearview Mirror" by going to the back of the book and defining your super objective.

Energy = Success

Mary Kay De La Matias, a licensed clinical counselor in Zanesville, Ohio, told me that energy, not money, is the key to one's success. And knowing that our super objective gives us energy, it is why we do what we do. And how important is the energy we generate? It will determine our successes and failures.

We all want to be around people who have good energy, who make us feel good about ourselves and others during our interaction. The more positive energy people have, the more success they will have in business, in relationships, and at work.

Think about the people you like to be around and what type of energy they have? The more energy individuals have, the more likely you want them in your circle, at your office, or part of your team.

And energy can't be faked — some individuals who are "over the top" on their energy are too much to handle, and they come off as inauthentic. The energy we exhibit needs to be real, genuine, and comes from a good place.

Once we tap into our super objective, we gain energy. When we find the cause, event, mission, or purpose that moves us, awakens us, and makes us feel alive, then we have found our passion.

UNLEASHING YOUR INNER MICHELANGELO:

"Lord, grant that I may always desire more than I can accomplish."
—Michelangelo

Contrarians having a greater chance of escaping the "Box"

Contrarians not only know what they want in life (super objective); they also question it. Contrarian thinkers have a greater chance of breaking free from the herd mentality by taking the opposite sides of issues, going for risks, and allowing themselves to think and act different.

Contrarian thinkers are trailblazers in business. They are the polarizing visionaries who are just as likely to be called crazy as brilliant, and they have the foresight to see hidden opportunities and seize them at just the right moment. (–Inc.com).

Four major examples of contrarians thinking outside the box include how they communicate, take risks, invest and consider politics.

Contrarians think different in regard to communication; they know that the "words mean nothing" and what is important is how we communicate non-verbally. More than 85% of communication is communicated non-verbally. However, the majority of people focus strictly on the words.

Contrarians think differently in regard to investing and know that mutual funds over time are a poor investment choice due to the fees associated with them, so they chose index funds instead. Index funds typically perform much better than mutual funds with a much lower fee. However, the majority of working Americans have their 401K/Retirement plan in mutual funds.

Contrarians think different in regard to politics, knowing that two political parties do not represent tens of millions of Americans' views. They chose not to be labeled by a party. Independents or no party affiliation can express views that don't fall into the labels of being a Democrat or Republican. However, the majority of Americans are registered as a Democrat or Republican.

Contrarians think different in regard to risk-taking and know that if one is to excel, one must take risks, which will include making mistakes. Risk-takers know that the only way one is going to gain a big reward is by taking a big risk. However, the majority of people avoid risks at all costs for fear of failing.

Just because one thinks like a contrarian doesn't mean they will be out of the proverbial box of life. However, it does mean that they are thinking about other options rather than following the masses and the herd mentality, which is a big step to getting out of the "Box."

Being a contrarian not only allows us to escape the box of life, it also helps us identify our super objective. Questioning your beliefs and challenging your mindsets are vital if we are truly going to uncover our super objective in life.

UNLEASHING YOUR INNER MICHELANGELO

"Genius is eternal patience."

–Michelangelo

Distinguishing Between Dreams vs. Needs

When you discover your super objective in life, you can begin to dream! Sonya Manchanda, a co-founder of Idiom, said, "Ask people about their needs, and they will give you a long list, one that varies from day to day and week to week. Ask people about their dreams and they'll give you just one answer, maybe two. It's not a list but a revealing look into what is truly meaningful in their lives."

I have needs that includes making more money, moving into a nicer neighborhood, starting a family, giving more money to charity, attending church on a weekly basis, and the list goes on and on. And not only does the list go on and on, it also changes from week to week.

One week, I feel I need more time in church, and the next week I feel I need to book more speaking gigs. While the following week I may feel I need to volunteer more of my time to a worthy cause. My needs seem to never be satisfied and are constantly changing.

However, I only have a couple of dreams with the main being to motivate people. For as long as I can remember, I have wanted to be a motivational speaker and inspire others to do more and achieve more. The idea of getting in front of a crowd and inspiring them is what gives me meaning, satisfaction, and purpose to what I do.

When someone writes me a thank-you note, sends me an email, or responds to one of my blogs, I truly feel blessed to have an opportunity to affect that individual's thinking. My dreams, unlike my needs, are constant and don't change week by week; rather, they last for decades.

UNLEASHING YOUR INNER MICHELANGELO:

"I saw the angel in the marble and carved until I set him free."
–Michelangelo

"Shoe Dog"

I am currently reading an autobiography on Phil Knight, the founder of Nike, titled "Shoe Dog." The term shoe dog is defined in the text as people who devoted themselves wholly to the making, selling, buying or designing of shoes. It's written that:

"Shoe Dogs" were people who devoted themselves wholly to the making, selling, buying or designing of shoes. Lifers used the phrase cheerfully to describe other lifers, men and women who had toiled so long and hard in the shoe trade, they thought and talked about nothing else. It was an all-consuming mania, a recognizable psychological disorder, to care so much about insole and outsoles, linings and welts, rivets and wamps.

As I am reading this book, I realize we all need to find the "Shoe Dog" in us! The "Shoe Dog" represents our passion, our purpose, and our super objective. It's the one thing we can't live without. My "Shoe Dog" is motivational speaking. I think about it all day and night, from writing blogs, to shooting videos, to updating my demo reel, to practicing new material for my presentations. It is all-consuming and occupies my whole day.

If you don't have a "Shoe Dog," create one by volunteering, starting a new hobby, or joining a group or association. You must find what burns inside you consume you in order to feel alive.

UNLEASHING YOUR INNER MICHELANGELO

"If people knew how hard I worked to get my mastery, it wouldn't seem so wonderful at all."

–Michelangelo

CHAPTER SUMMARY
Unleashing Your Inner Michelangelo

Michelangelo defined his super objective early in life and spent the rest of his life chasing it. His super objective was not just being sculptor, but being the best sculptor possible. I was speaking in Jackson, Mississippi, and I heard an architect talking about Michelangelo during his roundtable discussion. He said what made Michelangelo such an incredible artist was his ability to deliver clear and concise messages in his artwork, specifically, his sculptures.

Michelangelo would continue and continue to chip away at his sculptures until he got the image, and message he wanted to convey to his audiences. Take a look at a Michelangelo's famous sculpture the "David." It is a piece of artwork that delivers a clear and concise message of a man who is going to defeat Goliath using his superior skill and bravery.

Whenever I speak, I boil my presentations down to a single-point message to be clear and concise in my work. Everything in my talk revolves around a single point, a main message I want the group to take from my talk. If the material in my presentation doesn't support my main message, I delete it and find new material that does.

How many presentations have you sat through that go on and on with no point or direction, and are all over the board? This is the norm for me; it is rare to hear a talk, presentation, or program that is focused, clear, concise, and revolves around a main theme or point. However, when we present, perform, or create a piece of artwork, we must remember that our message needs to be clear, concise, and to the point if we want to make an impact on an audience.

Our super objective is about being specific and on point. We must be specific on what we want out of life and boil it down to a single-point message. We must determine one thing in life that we want to do and pour our heart and soul into it if we want to live up to our full potential.

THROUGH LINE

"Remember there are no small parts, only small actors."

The "Through Line" is created from our short term and long term objectives. Our multiple one to three year goals and our ultimate super objective combine into creating our through line, which includes:

- **Objectives (Multiple):** 1–3 year goals
- **Super Objective (One):** 5–50 year goal/ Ultimate purpose
- **Through Line:** Objectives and super objective combined

And once you create your "Through Line" in life, you can fail, make mistakes, dismantle patterns and routines, and most importantly, be yourself. I began constructing my "Through Line" in college when I declared theater as my major.

Before my senior year of college, I went back to my hometown of Zanesville, Ohio, and I directed the play "Inherit the Wind" at my school. At the time, West Muskingum High School didn't have a drama department, so we made one. We held auditions, cast the play, and used the gymnasium as the stage for our performance.

"Inherit the Wind" is a large cast with more than 20 actors. I ended up getting 22 students cast in this play. The play centers around Darwinism and the debate between evolution and the meaning of God. In my cast, I remember I had a student named Beau who played a couple of minor roles in the play; townsperson/juror.

Every time I watched my students rehearse, my eyes would be on Beau. He wouldn't even have any lines, but I would watch him on stage as he performed his actions with truth and sincerity. He knew what he wanted to accomplish in the scene. He didn't care that he had a small part and few lines, he was grateful to be on stage.

We should be like Beau, whether we have what we believe to be a small part or large part in life, because all the parts matter to the whole.

"Inherit the Wind" would not have been the play it was without Beau in it and the world we live in would not be the same without you in it. By creating a "Through Line" we give our lives purpose, direction and impact for ourselves and others.

Creating Your Through Line

Once you have defined your objectives and super objectives, the question is do they align? Do they go in the same direction? Many of us have no idea what we want in life short or long term, so we flounder. Even those who have defined goals may still have problems, because those objectives and super objectives do not align together.

The objectives and super objectives should be aligned and going in the same direction for our "Through Line" to form. My current short term objectives are to motivate and inspire audiences, write another book and partner my acting studio with a local theater company. My long term super objective is to become an international speaker.

My super objective is to be an international speaker. Regardless of the size of the crowd, I truly want to spark some new idea in their life, some new technique, or touch them with a personal story that hits home for them. My ultimate goal is to make an impact on the way someone thinks and acts in their life after they listen to me talk.

I need to check and see if my objectives align with my super objective to influence people and become and international speaker. If I motivate and inspire audiences it will lead me to speak to larger and larger crowds, which would help me achieve my super objective. The more books I write, the more people I can reach and influence, so that aligns with my super objective. By joining my acting studio with the theater company it will allow me to focus more on the other two short term goals, which we know already play into my super objective.

As you can see, all my objectives align with super objective, which gives me a strong "Through Line." As you discover your objectives and super objective, you need to make sure they align. Many people create smaller objectives that are not in alignment with their super objective.

Let me share a second example with you of a recruiter in working America. It doesn't matter what job you perform, the key is to create your "Through Line" in life. The short term objectives of a recruiter are to prepare candidates for interviews, create jobs leads that fit candidates and place candidates with jobs that will provide them a good living. All this funnels into the super objective of making a difference in people's lives, which helping them find the right career for them can certainly do.

As you can see, the objectives and super objectives align for a recruiter, and they have their "Through Line" in life. Take your time and define your objectives and super objective, and then see whether they align. Once you create your "Through Line" in life, you can take chances, dismantle patterns and routines, seek truth, and play the real you on the stage of life.

THE "THROUGH LINE" OF LIFE

"Doubt is the enemy of creativeness."

–Konstantin Stanislavski

Finish "Ripping Off the Rearview Mirror" by going to the back of the book and checking your "Through Line."

Failing Fast

People who know their "Through Line" in life are not only free to fail, but usually do so very fast. Once we have our direction in life, we can take chances, make mistakes, and fail. Because we know we are on the right track and any obstacles or challenges won't cause us to quit or give up. This energy and drive will offset any failures and mistakes, because we use them as learning lessons.

The cornerstone of experimentation and explorations is creativity, so allowing ourselves the opportunity to fail is key to fully experimenting and exploring. Creativity hinges on these two pillars and when one experiments and explores failure will undoubtedly be part of the process. The key is to embrace failure, but do it fast. Marissa Mayer, Chief Executive Officer for Yahoo, once talked about the concept of failing fast. She said, "It's totally okay to fail."

The key is to mitigate, contain, learn, and move on from one's failure. The problem for many of us is that we stay in the failure and never move on from it, or at least not fast enough. Failing fast allows us to try new things quickly and move on to the next idea, concept, or invention, even if it doesn't work.

Before I speak, whether it be a keynote address or workshop, I allow myself to fail. I allow myself to get on stage and make mistakes, take chances, and be wrong, and this mindset is crucial in the successes I have had as a speaker. Failures include improvisational sketches going wrong, videos not playing, having questions in my Q & A portion that I couldn't answer, and not being able to moonwalk.

In the fall of 2017, I spoke in Lincolnshire, Illinois. At the end of my address, I played a Michael Jackson video and attempted to moonwalk across the stage. I was terrible at it. However, the audience loved that I tried it and it received a big laugh. I might have failed, but it was a failure that engaged the audience and encouraged them to take their own risks regardless of failure.

Once you create your "Through Line" in life, quit being a perfectionist. If you allow yourself to be imperfect, make mistakes and fail, you will see your life open up as you never have before. Failing and failing fast is a key to living a creative life.

THE "THROUGH LINE" OF LIFE

"The greatest wisdom is to realize one's lack of it."
–Konstantin Stanislavski

Creating Pattern Disruptors

Knowing you're on the right path with your "Through Line" allows you to break your patterns and routines. Many people live a life filled with structure, predictability, and endless amounts of patterns and routines. Patterns and routines lead to predictability, comfortableness, and complacency. Only when we disrupt our patterns and routines do we change our perspectives, generate new ideas, and find our forgotten passions.

Two years ago, I took a trip overseas with my wife, and upon returning my outlook on work and life was changed. What I worried about before seemed trivial, and I realized how short life is and that we truly must seize the moment if we want to live a life without regrets. I am seizing the moment by getting up earlier in the morning to start my workday, which will leave more time in the afternoon to work out and read books into the early evening. In the past, I would make excuses to not put in extra work, avoid the gym, and watch TV rather than read.

During the flight home, I generated an incredible amount of ideas regarding the two businesses I run. As mentioned earlier, I have an acting studio and am a motivational speaker. I thought of new innovative ways to market my businesses, new strategies for success and additional classes for the acting studio. I generated more ideas on this flight than I had the month prior to our trip.

Passions are buried deep inside ourselves, and they will never be uncovered if we remain captive to our patterns and routines. The idea that we will discover what we love to do while going through the motions of daily life is highly unlikely. We need to change our setting, circumstances, and points of view if we are to change ourselves and uncover what we truly want in life.

There are many ways to disrupt one's pattern, but, I believe changing one's location is key. This could include going camping for a weekend, hiking in the woods, or taking a weekend trip by oneself. The key is to be in a new environment where one has time to think, reflect, and re-analyze one's goals in life. People who don't have a "Through Line" in life are prisoners to patterns and routines in that they are living their life looking back at it rather than seizing the present moment.

THE "THROUGH LINE" OF LIFE

"But keeping breaking traditions, I beg you."
–Konstantin Stanislavski

Seeking Truth

I have been told that we are three to seven answers away from the truth by multiple individuals who work in sales. I take this one step further by saying this is not only true for sales, but situations in life where we want to say no yet feel we can't. For any given situation, I usually don't say no at first to be polite, then I don't want to say it in order to avoid confrontation. I eventually feel worn down and say no in order to end the situation. A prime example is when I receive a sales call, something we can probably all relate to.

The first time a new place call me I usually say it's not a good time and ask them to call back later. We schedule a call and I never put it on my calendar, because I hope it won't happen. When the second call does come in, I usually recognize the number and let it go to voicemail. I know I need to tell the person no, but I can't pull the trigger because I don't want to hurt their feelings. Finally, on the third call I will answer and say I'm not interested in whatever they're selling. It takes me three calls to get to the truth of "no."

Ironically, I'm on the other end of this type of call as I'm always cold calling employers about my motivational speaking business. In my experience doing this, I appreciate the few clients who are direct with me. The few businesses I call and say no upfront I can respect and I always thank the person for their time. The individual on the other end of the line is usually surprised by this, because they just said "No" to me.

However, I want them to know I appreciate them not wasting my time while trying to be polite about it. I know the truth, I thank them for their time, their directness and wish them best of luck on their search for a speaker.

What I have learned is that trying to be polite, kind, or to avoid hurting someone's feelings does more harm than good. In the end, we all want the truth, directness, and honesty; yet we run from it. I am making it a practice to say what I mean and mean what I say not only on sales calls, but in all aspects of my life. I have noticed the more I do this, the better I communicate, the less time I waste for both parties involved, and the more I get accomplished.

My goal is to be one answer from the truth, which keeps me on my "Through Line" in life. Seeking truth sets us free and keeps us free from distractions, living in a false reality, and being consumed by "Noise." I find it impossible to stay on our "Through Line" in life if we are living in a world of lies or a false reality.

THE "THROUGH LINE" OF LIFE

"Unless the theater can ennoble you, make you a better person, you should flee from it."

–Konstantin Stanislavski

Do Something Different

Operating outside the box of life is all about trying something different. Our "Through Line" in life gives us confidence to do something different. Yes, it may or may not work, but that is what creativity is all about. The enemy of creativity is patterns and routines, and when we get stuck in them, we resist change and struggle with fear.

Here are some examples:

A real estate agent that relies on the MLS/Craigslist for marketing isn't trying something different. They are doing what most other agents do and nothing different. However, the real estate agent that calls friends and family members, has private showings and places ads on park benches is trying something different and that's the type of agent you should want working for you.

A teacher that relies on specific lesson plans, handouts and busy work for their students isn't trying something different. They are doing what most other teachers do, following a routine that isn't different from any other teacher. However, the teacher that engages their students with activities and games throughout the school day as a supplement to the curriculum is trying something different and that is the type of teacher you should want your child to be with.

A mom or dad that gets up, goes to work, comes home and goes to bed isn't trying something different. They are doing what most parents do and nothing different. However, the parent that goes dirt bike riding or any crazy activity you can think of with their child is doing something different and that is the parent that will create lasting memories with their children.

Regardless of our occupation, we can all be that different than the rest real estate agent, teacher or parent if we break our patterns and routines and create our "Through Line" in life.

THE "THROUGH LINE" OF LIFE:

"Love the art in yourself and not yourself in the art."
–Konstantin Stanislavski

Be Yourself; Everyone Else is Already Taken

The "Through Line" allows us to be us since we are going after what we want in life. We all hear the catch phrases to be authentic, be true to yourself and say what you mean and mean what you say. I take it one step further by adding "discover your viewpoint." This is your views on religion, finances, work and politics. Once we establish our point of view on issues, causes and conflicts our true identity emerges.

Recently, I have created stronger points of view on things that matter to me with faith, family, finances, politics and charity. My wife and I pray before every meal we eat. First, we are thankful for the food we eat and the blessings we have. Second, we want our daughter to grow up in a faith based house.

As for finances, she and I ascribe to the notion of keeping our debt down. We don't want to be debt slaves. Again, we aren't perfect and we have some debt, but we don't want our debt to dictate our future. We don't want to be paying interest for the rest of our lives or renting and never owning. This is a strong point of view both of us share.

In the political arena, I am becoming an independent. I believe it is hard to have an open and flexible line of thinking when we have to ascribe to a certain political affiliation. The idea that I will believe everything my party stands for on a wide range of issues from education to health care to the deficit is unimaginable.

I may agree with one party when it comes to health care, another party on immigration, and a third on the deficit. I want my own point of view that isn't boxed in by two political parties that I have to conform too.

What is your point of view on faith, finances and politics? Do you share them openly and honestly? If the answer is no, your viewpoint isn't being heard or recognized and you most likely haven't take the time to create your "Through Line" in life.

THE "THROUGH LINE" OF LIFE

"The main factor in any form of creativeness is the life of the human spirit."

–Konstantin Stanislavski

"A Lifeguard Not Knowing How to Swim"

Imagine a lifeguard not knowing how to swim.[2] They have all the knowledge and training, but they can't deliver when they jump in the pool because they don't know how to swim. The same could be said for all of us who do presentations and have all the knowledge and training, but can't communicate our message clearly and effectively.

How much time do you work on the content of your presentation with slides, materials, stats and quotes? How much time do you practice it in pace, timing, humor, energy and delivering a clear and concise message?

I spoke to teachers and administrators for schools in Ohio and Michigan and during my talk I said, "It doesn't matter what you know if you don't present effectively." This means students will check out of your lesson if you are unenthused and non-engaging.

This was my experience in college in that most teachers were intelligent and well-intentioned, but they didn't practice their presentations prior to class. As a result, their delivery was low energy, disengaging and there was very little student engagement. The instructors relied on PowerPoint slides as a means of communication.

During your next presentation at work or in the classroom what do you put priority on? Is it the material, the presentation, or both? Remember, in order for us to communicate clearly and effectively to audiences we must practice our material.

I would draw a similar conclusion to men and women in life who haven't taken the time to determine their "Through Line." If we don't define our objectives we will be like a lifeguard who can't swim and a presenter who hasn't practiced in that when the time comes we will not be ready to perform up to our full capability.

---

[2] Ken Lazar, created this quote, "A lifeguard not knowing how to swim" during an unplanned collaboration.

Remember there are no small parts, only small actors

We live in a time where negative thoughts and opinions appear to be true and positive thinking is false. Think how far we have come in our thinking. The general consensus is that politicians do nothing, the stock market is rigged, the real estate market is inflated, Democrats want to tax the wealthy and create socialism and Republicans want to cut taxes for the wealthy. The list of negatives assumption of our society goes on and on.

The question is when did we become so negative and jaded? Part of the answer lies within us and our mindsets. Our negative mindset attributes to the world we live in and create. We build and add to a negative reality when we think all politicians are crooked, when we take money out of the stock market because we think it is rigged, or when we label men and women according to their political party.

I met a politician during a breakfast event where he and I spoke at in Zanesville, Ohio. He acted like he knew me for years. He asked about my mom, my brother and sister and he knew their names. He went on to ask me how I was doing with the loss of my dad. Here is a man that took the time to look up the names of my brother and sister before the event and sincerely wanted to know how we were all doing with the loss of our father.

Negative thinking would say he is a politician and he wanted my vote. Truth is I live in Columbus, Ohio, and I am not in his district. I couldn't vote for him if I wanted to. Negative thinking would say he was only doing research on my family to make a good impression on his audience. The truth is he asked me all these questions in private.

We no longer think about the positive attributes of men and women rather, their motives and what they want from us. We have been taught to trust no one, fend for ourselves and believe everyone is out to get us. We think everyone has an agenda and a motive and if we aren't on guard we could be taken advantage of.

We can't change society or social media, but we can choose the "Through Line" we want to create in our lives. Regardless of all the negativity going on around us, we can make a positive impact on all who we come in contact with by doing what we want with the life we are living.

MINDSETS
"Orville Wright Didn't Have a Pilot's License"

Remember, Orville Wright didn't have a pilot's license, Kenny Chesney grew up with his humble east Tennessee roots, Tony Robbins had an abusive childhood and Konstantin Stanislavski's had severe self-doubt. However, they all had one thing in common and that was a "Through Line" in life whether they knew it or not or called it that or not.

If we can keep our "Through Line" in mind each and every day and have a mindset like Orville Wright, Tony Robbins, Kenny Chesney and Konstantin Stanislavski we can live up to up to our full potential.

We must stay on constant guard because if our mindset isn't correct it could destroy our "Through Line." The mindset has a huge impact on our "Through Line" and is affected by the internet, group thinking, money, fear and the people we associate with.

Let us begin with the biggest influencer of our mindset today which is the internet.

Search-Engine Mindset

Not only is "Noise" a distraction, it affects our mindsets. We are what we see on our search engines. What you search for on Google and Facebook or any other online site tracks our every movement and puts together an algorithm of our tendencies. If you like to buy gold coins and visit those websites, you will see banner ads on your social media pages for gold coins.

However, it goes deeper than just our buying habits. Many of us rely on social media for our news or one major broadcaster, whether that be ABC, Fox, NBC or CNN. This is what shapes our opinions, thoughts and beliefs. We let Facebook/ Twitter influence us on how we view the world, what we think of leaders, our political parties and our stance on controversial issues.

Influence is the key word. For many, if this is the only source of news one receives not only does that medium influence their thoughts, beliefs and opinions on a range of issues; it determines it.

What I do to break my "Search Engine Mentality" is find news outlets that are completely anti-mainstream. I am looking for opinions on the world that are outside of social media and the media conglomerates which include: ZeroHedge.com.

There are many alternative outlets out there and they all have their own agenda. However, ZeroHedge.com gives me a different point of view to help form my opinions. I share this site to show you how different these views are compared to mainstream news media.

Men and women who I admire, and respect are able to see and debate two sides of an issue, contrast points of view and then make decisions. In today's time it seems many of us have a single point of view and the other side of the issue doesn't exist, which comes from a "Search Engine Mindset."

ORVILLE WRIGHT DIDN'T HAVE A PILOT'S LICENSE

"If we all worked on the assumption that what is accepted as true is really true, there would be little hope of advance."

–Orville Wright

Better to Fail at Your Own Life than Live Someone Else's

I lived in Los Angeles for seven years and had a few successes, but many more failures. One of the successes I had was doing a commercial for Procter & Gamble that allowed me to get into the Screen Actors Guild. I remember during the orientation they told us this is the only union in the world where 2 percent of the union works. At that time, there were 98,000 union workers in L.A. and another 200,000 plus non-union actors going after a lot of the same roles.

Competition for parts was incredibly tough and this made many parts seemingly impossible to land. If you had money, connections, or an incredible talent you may have had a shot to audition for legitimate paid productions. Otherwise, you were auditioning for student films and low budget independent projects. I left L.A. almost 10 years ago.

When it comes to acting, you are competing against thousands of actors from all over the world. College degrees mean very little in Hollywood as your connections and look trump any education. You most likely will make just enough money to get by without insurance. The odds are you won't make it.

Regardless, I and only I wanted to be an actor and that is what caused me to move to L.A. to pursue a professional acting career. I was broke, rejected countless times and was uninsured, but it was still one of the happiest times in my life. Happiness doesn't necessarily come from success, but simply pursuing what one is passionate about.

When you discover your "Through Line" in life you live the life you want to live. You have defined your objectives, your super objective and that is where your focus and energies are going. If you don't have your "Through Line" in life defined, chances are you are living your life for someone else.

ORVILLE WRIGHT DIDN'T HAVE A PILOT'S LICENSE

"The airplane stays up because it doesn't have time to fall."
–Orville Wright

Running With the Herd

Running with the herd keeps us from creating a "Through Line" in life. I run with the herd, and my goal is to separate from it and think independent and original thoughts, which are the catalyst for creativity! I am reading a book titled *Think Like a Freak,* and this quote caught my attention:

"The first step is to appreciate that your opponent's opinion is likely based less on fact and logic than on ideology and herd thinking. If you were to suggest this to his face, he would of course deny it. He is operating from a set of biases he cannot see." Daniel Kahneman, Behavioral Psychologist

This is me at the polling booth. When I get to the polling booth I am not voting for the most qualified candidate or the one who embraces change, but the one who prescribes to the same general ideology I do from party affiliation.

For years I have voted on party lines and I didn't know one candidate from another. I voted blindly for a candidate that was in my herd. One could argue that those candidates share my values, beliefs and visions on certain issues, but this is exactly what "herd thinking" wants us to believe. It is not based on facts and logic, but an ideology. How do I know if they believe in what I believe in if I don't do research?

Two years ago, I stopped voting blindly for all candidates of a single party and began voting across party lines. The few candidates I knew I voted for and if I didn't know either candidate I would leave that part of the ballot blank. Recently, more and more of my ballot has been blank.

Currently, I see myself as an independent that votes both Democrat and Republican. For me, this is a way to break free from the herd and vote for the most qualified man or woman. Politics is the epicenter for herd thinking, is it any surprise that we have two major parties for a country of 318 million people?

Really, two parties represent 318 million people that is diverse and multicultural. The question isn't whether we are a Democrat or a Republican, the question is do we vote on logic and reason or on an ideology?

If you want to be honest with yourself, what is your party affiliation? Do you truly believe everything that your party stands for? The more we think like the pack the less likely we are to live the life we want to live which is driven by our "Through Line" in life.

ORVILLE WRIGHT DIDN'T HAVE A PILOT'S LICENSE

"No flying machine will ever fly from New York to Paris."
–Orville Wright

Self Worth = Net Worth

When my bank account is low on funds I take it personal and I think there is something wrong with me. I ask myself why don't I make more money? Am I lazy? Am I not working hard enough? All these questions go through my mind and I begin to doubt my talents, abilities and self-worth.

Only when I take a step back do I see that I have it wrong. I have an acting studio in Columbus, Ohio, where I teach acting classes to all ages.

I have had the studio for close to nine years. I realize the money I have made from the studio pales in comparison to the opportunity I have had to make an impact on the lives of these students.

Bringing youth out of their shell who are introverted and sit in the back of the classroom is a challenge I face every year. They lack confidence and self-esteem I must help them find. They're not just gaining basic acting skills, but a feeling of self-worth they didn't have before. Building their confidence while introducing them to the craft of acting is my objective.

Whether we are in a classroom, board room, conference room, office, patrolling the streets, or working at a construction zone we all have an opportunity to impact someone's life through our interactions and the relationships we create. The problem is we minimize the importance of relationships and interactions and think how we interact or treat people really doesn't matter.

Once we have properly defined what we want out of life our self-worth doesn't have to equal our net worth. The acting studio has taught me that my purpose in life goes well beyond my bank account.

ORVILLE WRIGHT DIDN'T HAVE A PILOT'S LICENSE

"We laid the track on a smooth stretch of ground about one hundred feet north of the new building."

–Orville Wright

You Are the Average of the 5 People You Spend the Most Time With[3]

Our mindsets are shaped by the people we spend time with. What five people do you spend the majority of your time with outside your family? Are you the average of those five people in regard to your social and economic status, work ethic, energy and drive? Our environment has a major impact on all aspects of our life and often times it is overlooked or minimized.

The five people I spend the most time with are those who share my office complex in Dublin, Ohio. Around my office is one person in the

---

[3] "You are the average of the five people you spend the most time with." –Jim Rohn

staffing industry, three people in the sales industry and one in the health care industry.

The gentleman in the staffing industry is the hardest worker in my circle of five. He gets in the office every day at 8 a.m. and leaves after 6 p.m. In addition, there are many days he works after normal business hours by going to various networking events and putting on events himself.

One of the sales people is on the other end of the spectrum. He makes it to the office two or three days out of the week and is unpredictable with his hours. I never know when I will see him at the office and which days of the week he will be there. As for the other three in my group they consistently work from 8 a.m. to 5 p.m. Monday to Friday, but rarely work extra hours. Once their day is finished at 5 p.m. they go home and end their workday.

So where do I fall? Right in the middle, I am the average of these five people. I don't work as hard as the gentleman in staffing, but I work more consistently than my friend in sales. This relates to the law of averages, which is the theory that the result of any given situation will be the average of all outcomes.

Now, that you have discovered your "Through Line" in life are you ready to challenge or change the five people you spend the most time with? Remember, we are the average of those five people and if you want to live up to your full potential it is imperative.

ORVILLE WRIGHT DIDN'T HAVE A PILOT'S LICENSE:

"The desire to fly is an idea handed down to us by our ancestors who, in their grueling travels across trackless lands in prehistoric times, looked enviously on the birds soaring freely through."

–Orville Wright

Immune to Rejection

What would your life look like if you didn't fear rejection? If making a mistake, failing, or falling short wasn't the end of the world? Would you start a new business or relationship?

I presented "Smash the Box" to a bank in Maryland a couple of weeks ago. A man there asked me what was my biggest take away from living seven years in Los Angeles. I told him I was immune to rejection.

While living in L.A. and pursuing work as an actor I auditioned for everything under the sun. I went out for commercials, films, television shows, college short films, industrial movies, print work; you name it. Most of the time I failed and didn't get the part. I got to a point where I didn't care if I received the part, I just wanted to give it my best effort.

When I left L.A. I created a mindset where I didn't fear rejection or failure. I was immune to rejection. This mindset got me into starting the three business I have now. I flip houses with my wife, work as a motivational speaker and run an acting studio. I love creating and building businesses and the fear of failure doesn't stop me from chasing my dreams.

You become immune to rejection by creating a mindset where you don't care what others think, you believe in yourself and abilities, and you stop seeking approval from others. You live the life you want to live and know that failing and rejection are part of the creative process. You tell yourself that you are immune to rejection because you are following your "Through Line" in life.

ORVILLE WRIGHT DIDN'T HAVE A PILOT'S LICENSE:

"No data on air propellers was available, but we had always understood that it was not a difficult matter to secure an efficiency of 50% with marine propellers."

–Orville Wright

What can we learn from Michael Jackson?

Michael Jackson had a mindset early on in life that allowed him to improvise. At his concerts you would see him yelling at his fans and telling them that he loved them. He would chant with them and exchange dialogue that wasn't planned.

The most memorable keynote address I delivered is when I had my own Michael Jackson moment and improvised. There were three parts of my presentation I improvised that wasn't part of my script. I disappeared at the opening, I presented in the middle of the room and performed improvisational sketches.

When the gentleman finished my introduction and said, "Here is Chad J. Willett" I quietly walked past him and the entire audience and exited the room without saying a word. I stayed out in the hallway for about 10 seconds and then reappeared to deliver the keynote address. When I reentered the room, the audience had a big laugh and it ended up being an ice breaker for me and the group.

I also presented in the middle of the room to connect with the audience that was sitting in the back, and let them know that they were part of this experience of "Smashing the Box." The audience appeared shocked to see their presenter speaking in the middle of the room during the presentation and not up front behind a podium.

Finally, I performed two improvisational sketches with audience members to demonstrate how one "Smashes the Box" personally and professionally. I believe it is one thing to talk about theories and techniques and another thing to put those techniques to a test in front of a live audience. I wanted to do the latter. Defining our "Through Line" will give us confidence to get off the script personally and professionally. When we are grounded in what we do and want out of life we can take risks, try something different and think outside the box of life.

CHAPTER SUMMARY
Orville Wright didn't have a pilot's license

We need to create an Orville Wright mindset if we want to "Rip Off the Rearview Mirror." Orville Wright exemplifies what "Ripping Off the Rearview Mirror" is all about. The innovator of aviation lived without fear, he went after his objectives and had a "Through Line" in life that defined his passion and purpose.

When he was out on the plains of Kitty Hawk, North Carolina, trying to get a pile of metal, bolts and wings up into the air and fly, he didn't ask for anyone's permission. He didn't wait to get a certification or receive a diploma, he just did it. His mindset was about experimentation, exploration and taking risks. This allowed him to do the impossible and fly.

I tried to take on Orville Wright's mindset when I became a motivational speaker. People always ask me how do you become a motivational speaker? They ask if there are classes to take, seminars to attend and certifications to receive. You can do all those things or you can be like Orville Wright and just do it.

I have a passion for speaking. I feel blessed to have an opportunity to motivate and inspire individuals and be a part of their journey in life. My first speaking gig was a keynote address on creative leadership where I used principles from my acting studio to create a one-hour keynote address. I didn't know exactly what I was doing or how it turned out, but I didn't let fear keep me from trying.

Your adventure may not be flying a plane or motivational speaking, but your passions and quest for life are within you and only you know what they are. More importantly, allow yourself to pursue them without asking for permission, or seeking a piece of paper that gives you the validation to try something new and exciting. We live in a time where everything must be planned out, certified and double checked. This endless need for approval and validation impedes our ability to create and innovate. Rather than waiting for approval, dive in and begin your next adventure.

Do you need permission to try new things or do you just do it? Those who "Rip Off the Rearview Mirror" just do it.

"Objectives" Worksheet

Define your short term objectives (1-3 years from now):

Objective #1:
_____
_____
_____
_____
_____

Objective #2:
_____
_____
_____
_____
_____

Objective #3:
_____
_____
_____
_____
_____

Only define 3 objectives you want to accomplish in the next 1-3 years.

"Super Objective" Worksheet

Define your super objectives (5 + years from now):

Super Objective #1:

_____

_____

_____

_____

_____

_____

_____

_____

_____

_____

_____

_____

_____

_____

_____

*Only define 1 super objectives that you want to accomplish in next 5 + years.

"Through Line" Worksheet

Do your objectives and super objective align with one another?

Objective #1: _____

_____

_____

Objective #2: _____

_____

_____

Objective #3: _____

_____

_____

Super Objective #1: _____

_____

_____

You have created your "Through Line" in life. Focus on your "Through Line" in life and you will "Rip Off the Rearview Mirror!"

Thank You

I want to thank my savior, Jesus Christ, and our heavenly father for allowing me to meet the love of my life, my wife, Erika Willett. I am forever blessed to have met such a wonderful, loving and caring woman. Our daughter, Scarlett, is the light of our world and we can't wait to see how her life unfolds.

My mom, Mary Kay Willett, is an inspiration of how to truly live life outside the box of life. My dad, Lynn H. Willett, was a great man who dedicated his life to higher education at Elgin Community College and Zane State College.

My brother, Jason, gave the greatest best man speech ever at our wedding, in Spanish and English. I feel blessed to have memories with my sister, Allison, at the University of Kentucky and Ohio University. I also want to thank my sister-in-law, Jennifer Beck Willett, and brother-in-law, Mike Tominc, for being a part of the Willett family.

Finally, I want to thank my wife's family who have also become my own in Texas and Mexico. They include Julian and Ninfa Castillo Arroyo, Angel and Elvira Barrera, and Julian and Eva Castillo Arroyo. My family down south knows how to live life to the fullest.

Notes

Chapter 1

1. Kenny Chesney; Ross Copperman; Shane McAnally; Jon Nite songwriters of "Noise"
2. Randy Pausch- A computer science professor at Carnegie Mellon. Presentation titled, "The Last Lecture"

Chapter 2

1. Tony Robbins- Motivational Speaker. Credited with the quote "Where our focus goes energy flows."
2. Simon Senek- Author/ Motivational Speaker. Creator of the "Why" TED Talk
3. Ken Lazar- Founder of Ability Professional Network. Credited with the quote "Unbalance = Success"
4. Muhammad Ali- Boxing Great. Credited with the quote, "I am the greatest."
5. Soichoro Honda- Founder of Honda. Credited with the quote, "Kickout the Ladder"
6. Erik Wahl- Graffiti Artist. Author of "Unthink"

Chapter 3

1. Michelangelo- Sculptor.
2. Deacon Roger Minner- Deacon at St. Mary's Church in German Village
3. Sonya Manchada- Co-founder of Idiom.
4. Phil Knight- Author of "Shoe Dog"

Chapter 4

1. "Inherit the Wind"- Written by Jerome Lawrence and Robert E. Lee

2. CATCO- Theater company Columbus, Ohio

3. Broadway2LA Acting Studio- Acting studio Columbus, Ohio

4. Konstantin Stanislavski- Russian director.

5. Marissa Meyer- CEO of Yahoo. Credited with "Fail Fast"

6. Mary Kay De La Matias- Professional counselor in Zanesville, Ohio

Chapter 5

1. ZeroHedge- Informational website

2. Orville Wright- Pilot.

3. Screen Actor's Guild- Union for actors.

4. Daniel Kahneman- Behavioral therapist.

5. Jim Rohn- TV personality. Credited with you are the "Average of the 5 People You Associate With"

6. Michael Jackson- Singer/ Songwriter

Index

About the Author

Chad J. Willett (NSA/SAG-AFTRA/MA) spent 7 years in Los Angeles as a professional actor which includes training at the world famous improvisational school, "The Groundlings." He was featured in the hit films "She's All That" with Paul Walker, "Halloween H20," with Jamie Lee Curtis, and "Can't Hardly Wait" with Jennifer Love Hewitt.

Chad has also worked for three Fortune 500 companies and is an entrepreneur: Manpower, ITT Technical Institute, and the Washington Post and is the owner/operator of Broadway2LA Acting Studio. He leverages his acting background with his experience in working America to create one-of-a-kind keynote addresses/workshops for his audiences.

He inspires audiences to unleash their creative energies by SMASHING concepts, walls, barriers, and in short…the Box of life! He also writes a weekly blog where he challenges traditional and self-limiting lines of thinking.

Chad is a member of St. Mary's Church in German Village, Ohio and the creator of "Make Faith Matter." He has also been involved with "Big Brothers, Big Sisters," and a reading literacy program for adults. Finally, Chad is married to his wife Erika, and is a proud father to his baby girl, Scarlett.

Additional Reading Material

Order "Smash the Box"

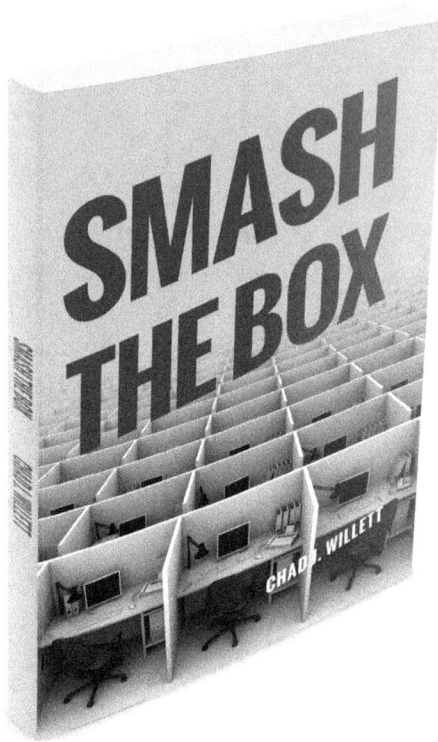

Readers will **"SMASH"** their concept of how books are read by reading a book that has:

- Pages upside down
- No table of contents
- No page numbers
- Pages out of order

Be prepared to "SMASH" the way you read books! **"Smash the Box"** unlocks our creative energies through 4 simple techniques that gets us out of our head (Mental Prison) and into a creative space.

Order Online: https://chadjwillett.com/shop/

www.ingramcontent.com/pod-product-compliance
Lightning Source LLC
LaVergne TN
LVHW051209080426
835512LV00019B/3178